LENT AND MISSIONS

A 40-Day Devotional

LENT AND MISSIONS

A 40-Day Devotional

Bradley Bell and Nathan Sloan

© 2023 BY BRADLEY BELL AND NATHAN SLOAN

All rights reserved. Except for brief quotations in critical publications or review, no part of this book may be reproduced in any manner without prior written permission from the publisher. Write to:

Permissions, The Upstream Collective
P.O. Box 23871
Knoxville, TN 37933

www.theupstreamcollective.org

ISBN: 978-1-7343705-9-1

Printed in the United States of America

Scripture quotations, unless otherwise indicated, are from the ESV® Bible (The Holy Bible, English Standard Version®), copyright © 2001 by Crossway, a publishing ministry of Good News Publishers. Used by permission. All rights reserved.

Editor: David McWhite
Cover and Interior design: Hayley Moss, Moss Photo and Design, LLC
hayleyrmoss@gmail.com
Cover images courtesy of Matt Herp
All other images courtesy of Unsplash.com

To Sojourn Church Midtown, for whom we originally wrote this book as fellow missions pastors. Thank you for shaping our understanding of the gospel, God's mission to the world, and the beauty of the historical church calendar.

TABLE OF CONTENTS

Introduction	9
Fasting Guide	13
Day 1	15
Day 2	16
Day 3	17
Day 4	18
Day 5	21
Day 6	22
Day 7	23
Day 8	24
Day 9	25
Day 10	26
Day 11	29
Day 12	30
Day 13	31
Day 14	32
Day 15	33
Day 16	34
Day 17	37
Day 18	38
Day 19	39
Day 20	40
Day 21	41
Day 22	42
Day 23	45
Day 24	46
Day 25	47
Day 26	48
Day 27	49
Day 28	50
Day 29	53

Day 30 54
Day 31 55
Day 32 56
Day 33 57
Day 34 58
Day 35 61
Day 36 62
Day 37 63
Day 38 64
Day 39 65
Day 40 66
Next Steps & Resources 68
Acknowledgments 70
About the Authors 71
Other Books from Upstream 72

INTRODUCTION

Behold, the Lamb of God, who takes away the sin of the world!

John 1:29

If you've ever climbed a mountain, then you know the struggle. As you begin your journey, the cool morning air fills your lungs with anticipation, and the trail seems smooth and inviting. Then, at some point along the way, perhaps because of the elevation or weather or hunger, a weariness sets in. Slowly, each step becomes a reconsideration.

A hard trail forces you to be honest with yourself. Can you make it to the top? You long for that precious last turn when the peak finally comes into view. Your legs may be mush, but if you stick with it, beholding such a sight suddenly strengthens them with defiant joy. From there on, every step becomes a declaration: *You are ready to summit.*

John the Baptist knew a hard trail. And he also beheld the greatest summit in all creation. Towering high over the whole Bible is the life, death, and resurrection of Jesus Christ, the Lamb of God. From the garments of skin God made to cover Adam and Eve after they sinned against him (Genesis 3:21) to the Jewish sacrificial system that called for the slaughter of male lambs without blemish (Leviticus 1:3), everything before Christ looked forward to his coming to take away the sin of the world. Then, from the pouring out of the Holy Spirit at Pentecost by "Christ our Passover lamb" (1 Corinthians 5:7) to the people gathered around that Lamb who have been ransomed from every nation, tribe, people, and language (Revelation 7:9), everything after Christ looks back to all that he accomplished.

John the Baptist stood before *this* summit, and he was sent to prepare others for the way up. Yet the people of Israel were stumbling over their own desires. Their eyes were searching for a revolutionary leader who would put them back on top. No wonder they missed the point when John said, "Behold, the Lamb of God, who takes away the sin of the world"—no one was looking for that kind of messiah. Who saw it coming that a man of sorrows would suffer and die to bring salvation not only to the Jews but to people all over the world? This is why John's ministry was a call to repent. It was the only way to prepare the world for its Savior.

In the same way, the season of Lent is about preparation and repentance.

LENT AND MISSIONS

It is the forty days of the historical Christian calendar (not counting Sundays, which are traditionally reserved for public worship) stretching from Ash Wednesday to Easter. The practice of observing Lent began in the third and fourth centuries and was meant to point back to Israel's forty years of wandering in the wilderness and Jesus' forty days of fasting in the wilderness. In view of the full redemption story, both of these biblical events were formative acts of preparation for the fulfillment of God's promises. Lent is simply intended to shape us in a similar way. It is the time that Christians have historically set aside to make their hearts ready to remember Jesus' death and to celebrate Jesus' resurrection.

The tone of Lent is set by two significant days: Ash Wednesday and Good Friday. Ash Wednesday traditionally includes the imposition of ashes in the form of a cross on the forehead, often given with the declaration, "From dust you came, and to dust you shall return." Similarly, Good Friday bears the bittersweet recounting of Jesus' suffering and death, traditionally including a reading of the passion narrative and the extinguishing of candles. Thus, Lent gives us space to admit the struggle: though the defiant joy of Christ's victory is ours, it came at an unimaginably great cost; though our salvation is sealed forever, we still face mortality, indwelling sin, and a fallen world.

But there is more to this struggle.

If we who have hope are to pause for a season to lament sin and death, then should we not also lament for those who have no hope? There are billions who do not share in the victory of Easter. They are the people around us who have no one helping them understand their need for (and God's supply of) a Savior. And they are the people around the world who don't even have access to that kind of engagement. If we are going to prepare our hearts for Easter, then how much greater our celebration will be when we've been longing for *all people* to share in it with us!

For this reason we originally wrote this devotional in 2015 as missions pastors at Sojourn Community Church (now Sojourn Church Midtown) in Louisville, Kentucky. To be honest, "Lent and Missions" is a phrase we've never heard. The concepts do not naturally seem to overlap. But our desire was to change that for our church members. We wanted them to experience this special season with even greater significance. We wanted them to be formed even more deeply by God's global purpose for Easter.

INTRODUCTION

We wanted them to be sent into Pentecost (the season following Easter) with the same renewal and mission of the early church. And now we want that for you and your church too.

In this devotional you will find that each day follows a simple liturgical pattern: a Scripture reading, a brief reflection, and a prayer. The only variation is that each Friday (Days 3, 9, 15, 21, 27, 33, and 39) includes a call to fasting (see Fasting Guide). You will also notice that the Scripture readings progress from Genesis to Revelation, focusing on passages that uniquely reveal God's global mission. These selections and prayers are merely prompts; feel the freedom to read and pray more extensively, beyond what we have provided. On the other hand, you may find the brevity of content refreshing and welcome the opportunity simply to be still for thirty seconds in an otherwise frenzied day. Whatever you have to offer is welcome!

If you are a church leader, we encourage you to consider making this resource available to your entire church and calling them all to the Lenten season with prayer and fasting for missions. Since this devotional was originally written in the context of the local church and for that local church, we can testify to the impact of a congregation taking this climb together. It could profoundly change your church, its appreciation of the Christian calendar, and its participation in God's mission.

As two men who came from traditions that do not observe Lent, we feel it's important to acknowledge at the outset of this book that Lent is unfamiliar to many Christians. Some may even find it confusing in light of its varied practices and, in some cases, malpractices. We acknowledge that some may observe Lent as nominal Christians seeking a sense of righteousness through penance and fasting. Others may fail to clearly emphasize its culmination in Easter, making introspection an end in itself rather than beholding the glory of God in Christ. Despite its capacity for being misused and misunderstood, we believe the proper observance of Lent still has great usefulness for the church. We do not, however, wish to force this onto all readers, so please proceed as your conscience permits.

Friends, Easter is not only the summit of human history—it's the defining reality of the Christian life. This devotional is a guide for preparing our hearts for Easter. It's a climb toward the breathtaking panorama of what

Jesus has done for us. Our prayer is that in the days to come, the Lamb of God who took away your sin will allow you to behold him anew—"having the eyes of your hearts enlightened, that you may know what is the hope to which he has called you" (Ephesians 1:18)—that you may more joyfully participate in his global mission.

The risen Savior of the world is in sight. Let's prepare ourselves for him!

FASTING GUIDE

During these forty days of Lent leading up to Easter (not including Sundays), we encourage you to consider fasting on each Friday. Fasting is a lost discipline for many Christians, which is unfortunate since Jesus himself modeled it for us and commended it to us (Matthew 4:1–2; 6:16–18, 9:14–17). It has traditionally been practiced during Lent for a number of reasons, including the following:

Fasting creates opportunities for focused prayer. It can take the place of the time that we would otherwise commit to food preparation, eating, and cleaning up afterward. Rather than filling up this extra time with work, leisure, or simply brooding over our hunger, we are lavished with unhurried time before God.

Fasting provides a tangible way to experience our dependency. It may well expose how much we rely on food not simply for our bodies, but also for our emotional state. Although there may be some benefit to abstaining from things like sweets and social media, Lent has traditionally involved a food fast because of its unique power to reveal our continual need for God.

Fasting fosters concentration on God's sufficiency. It creates a heightened sense of spiritual awareness as we withdraw from the noise of our lives and go to God with our hunger. His invitation is to sit in his presence, empty to be filled (see Matthew 4:4). This is where our longing for food can become a homesickness for Jesus's return, the only thing that can truly satisfy us.

Fasting offers a way to grow in self-control. The busyness of our lives, especially during the excitement of spring's arrival, can easily lead us to bypass Easter with little thought. In order to be spiritually disciplined enough to prepare well for Easter, we need the fortitude that physical self-control builds. Fasting, then, is a mighty weapon in the fight against distraction and sin.

Fasting also has great relevance to global missions. For example, it was from a posture of worshiping and fasting that the church at Antioch first heard the Spirit calling them to send Barnabas and Saul (Acts 13:1–2). Amazingly, before they laid hands on them and sent them off, we read that the church fasted and prayed again (Acts 13:3). Furthermore, there are a number of historical missions movements that began with this kind of desperate prayer (take a moment and do a search for "Haystack Prayer Meeting" and "Moravian Hundred-Year Prayer Meeting"). Lent, then, gives us an opportunity to participate in a long legacy of missions-focused fasting.

For this reason, beginning with the first Friday (Day 3) after Ash Wednesday (Day 1) and continuing each Friday during Lent (Days 9, 15, 21, 27, 33, and 39), we invite you to fast, to literally hunger with longing, for the hope of Easter to bless the nations.

Of course, you will need to give consideration to physical limitations, such as pregnancy and diabetes. If not eating for a full day would jeopardize your health, then please consider fasting from something other than food. Also, although we recommend limiting what you drink (so as not to curb your hunger with extra fluids), we do not recommend dry fasting, wherein you also abstain from all fluids including water. This practice can be extremely dangerous and should be avoided. And finally, beware of overexerting yourself through exercise or manual labor on Fridays. It may even be wise to let your spouse or a friend know about your fast, in case you experience light-headedness or other complications throughout the day.

There are three basic ways to fast on Fridays:

1. A 36-hour food fast: after eating dinner on Thursday night, you don't eat again until breakfast Saturday morning.
2. A 24-hour food fast: after eating dinner on Thursday night, you don't eat again until dinner on Friday night.
3. A 12-hour food fast: after eating breakfast on Friday morning, you don't eat again until dinner on Friday night.

We will remind you of this guide each Friday and provide you with some specific prompts for that day's fasting. In the days to come, may you "not live by bread alone, but by every word that comes from the mouth of God" (Matthew 4:4).

DAY 1 | WEDNESDAY

READ PSALM 90

Before the mountains were brought forth, or ever you had formed the earth and the world, from everlasting to everlasting you are God. You return man to dust and say, "Return, O children of man!"

Psalm 90:2–3

Before the world existed, God was God, and God was God without us. The psalmist here confesses our total dependence, describing us as mere dirt waiting for the command to come to life or to pass away. We do well to recognize our desperate situation—we must own our ashes. Because humanity has fallen into sin, to ignore our mortality is to live in denial of the truth. Ash Wednesday is a raw, biblical confession of the truth: though our salvation is sure in Christ, we still face death, indwelling sin, and a world that is not what God intended it to be. And yet that is an infinitely better state than that of the many people among the nations who face those same realities, yet without hope. As is often spoken and sung on Ash Wednesday, "Lord, have mercy."

And he will have mercy. We can be sure of this because Jesus became flesh—he took on our dirt. More than giving his forehead for the sign of the cross, Jesus took the cross upon himself in full measure. Then, in rising from the dead, he brought beauty from ashes. The more fully we acknowledge our need for him, the more eager we are to receive him and to hold out his mercy to the unreached before they return to dust.

Prayer

Father, before the mountains were born or you brought forth the world, from everlasting to everlasting, you are God. I confess and remember that you are greater than me, because you were before me. As I journey through Lent, teach me to number my days. Give me a heart of wisdom, a heart that knows its need and clings to your provision in Christ. Lord, have mercy. Amen.

DAY 2 | THURSDAY

READ GENESIS 1

In the beginning, God created the heavens and the earth . . . And God blessed them. And God said to them, "Be fruitful and multiply and fill the earth and subdue it, and have dominion over the fish of the sea and over the birds of the heavens and over every living thing that moves on the earth."

Genesis 1:1, 28

Genesis 1:1 has been called the most pregnant verse in all the Bible. Simply put, everything began with God, and so it was all really good. It was the kind of good that should have filled up the whole world. You see, the Great Mandate (Genesis 1:28) is the foundational paradigm for all missiology. It calls God's people to live as his sent ones in every part of life, in every part of the world. It was Adam and Eve's commission to do this. And it's ours too.

Prayer

Father, I praise you because I am fearfully and wonderfully made. Your eyes saw my unformed body, and all the days ordained for me were written in your book before one of them came to be. Thank you for creating so well, and for sharing with me the task to fill your earth with good. Lord, may your earth be filled with the good knowledge of your glory as waters cover the sea. Amen.

DAY 3 | FRIDAY

READ GENESIS 3:1–13

Then the eyes of both were opened, and they knew that they were naked. And they sewed fig leaves together and made themselves loincloths. And they heard the sound of the Lord God walking in the garden in the cool of the day, and the man and his wife hid themselves from the presence of the Lord God among the trees of the garden.

Genesis 3:7–8

Even though Adam and Eve walked with God and had every good thing, they chose evil. They disregarded God and his good command, which is sin. Many scoff at this story, regarding it as mythical nonsense, but these are God's trustworthy words, and the proof is in us. We, too, disregard God's commands. From the womb, we are infected with the same rebellious nature as Adam and Eve. The world is broken. And it's our fault. Lent is not the time for shifting blame. Here, we recognize what led to Easter. Here, we confess our part.

Fasting & Prayer

Each Friday during Lent, we invite you to fast, to literally hunger with longing for the hope of Easter to bless the nations. See the Fasting Guide in the front of this devotional for helpful details. Begin this day by meditating on the story from Genesis 3. The Scriptures tell us that "in Adam all die" (1 Corinthians 15:22). Allow yourself to feel the tragedy of humanity's separation from God. Use your hunger pangs throughout the day to remember what it was like for you to be "without God in the world" (Ephesians 2:12). Let this time of reflection lead you to compassionate prayer for those who are still without him. Then end your fast with a good meal and rejoice in the hope of a coming Savior.

DAY 4 | SATURDAY

READ GENESIS 3:14–24

I will put enmity between you and the woman, and between your offspring and her offspring; he shall bruise your head, and you shall bruise his heel.

Genesis 3:15

This passage is full of both sobriety and hope. The skin coverings that God made for Adam and Eve foretell of a coming sacrificial Lamb. The flaming sword that guards the tree of life shows that God doesn't want Adam and Eve in their crippled state forever. And finally, God's death sentence for the serpent speaks of a coming Son of Man who would suffer in order to crush Satan's lying skull. If Lent feels somewhat morbid to you, then good—because Genesis 3 is morbid. It shows us just how serious God is about sin and how, from the beginning, he had personally committed to destroy it forever.

Prayer

Father, you do not take lightly the sins that I commit, because you are a God of holiness who loves justice. You never allow evil to go unpunished. I thank you for your wisdom and mercy in devising a plan to save people from every nation, tribe, people, and language—people like me—by sending your Son to take my death sentence. How can I thank you enough? Bless the Lord, O my soul! Amen.

SUNDAY

Sundays during Lent are not counted as part of the forty days because they are traditionally reserved for public worship. In order to provide space to focus on gathering with your local church, this book does not include a Sunday devotional. However, we do encourage you to read Scripture, pray, and practice other spiritual disciples as you see fit. The devotional will continue on Monday.

DAY 5 | MONDAY

READ GENESIS 4; 6:5–8

The Lord saw that the wickedness of man was great in the earth, and that every intention of the thoughts of his heart was only evil continually. And the Lord regretted that he had made man on the earth, and it grieved him to his heart.

Genesis 6:5–6

It's tough to take in the emotions expressed by God here. But we need to feel them. This passage doesn't suggest that God was any less in control or had changed his character; it just shows us he has a heart. He aches over the things worth aching over. The effect of sin had not only gone vertically—between God and man—but it had also gone horizontally—between man and woman. A wall of hostility had been built. Cain proved it, Lamech proved it, and then everyone in the world besides Noah proved it. Christ gave his life in order to tear down that wall (Ephesians 2:14), so imagine how much it grieves the heart of God to see so many among the nations who are not yet reconciled to one another in Christ.

Prayer

Father, there is no one good, not a single one. As I grow closer to you, I become more aware of the evil inclinations and thoughts of my heart. You have torn down the wall that separated me from you and your family, but I confess that I sometimes build walls back up. Forgive me, Lord. Let the words of this hymn be my prayer: "Nothing in my hand I bring, simply to Thy cross I cling; naked, come to Thee for dress; helpless, look to Thee for grace; foul, I to the fountain fly; wash me, Savior, or I die!" Amen.

DAY 6 | TUESDAY

READ GENESIS 11:1–9

So the Lord dispersed them from there over the face of all the earth, and they left off building the city. Therefore its name was called Babel, because there the Lord confused the language of all the earth. And from there the Lord dispersed them over the face of all the earth.

Genesis 11:8–9

The hope of a new start through Noah and his family was quickly extinguished as humanity grew in number again. At Babel, mankind gathers and builds a tower to prove that they don't need God. Like spiteful children, they not only refuse God's original commission to go and fill the earth (Genesis 1:28), but they do precisely the opposite. The confusion of their language might appear to be a strange judgment, but it is done according to a gracious plan: it fills the world with unique languages and cultures. Keep this in mind as the story continues to unfold.

Prayer

Father, there is a way that seems right to us, but in the end it leads to death. I confess that my thoughts are not your thoughts, and my ways are not your ways. Yet in every way I fail you, you are able to work through my failure for my good. This is true not only for me; it can also be true for anyone around the world who calls upon your name. I am humbled and hopeful because your anger lasts only a moment, but your favor lasts a lifetime. Amen.

DAY 7 | WEDNESDAY

READ JOSHUA 24:1–5, GENESIS 12:1–9

And I will make of you a great nation, and I will bless you and make your name great, so that you will be a blessing. I will bless those who bless you, and him who dishonors you I will curse, and in you all the families of the earth shall be blessed.

Genesis 12:2–3

When God chose Abraham, Joshua tells us in an overlooked comment that he was an average person worshiping false gods (Joshua 24:2). Some people assume Abraham was chosen because God saw his remarkable faith, but it's actually the opposite. Purely by grace did God choose this pagan to be a blessing to all peoples through his offspring.

Are we any different? Did we catch God's attention in some special way? Absolutely not! Lent reminds us of the days in which we were worshiping false gods and living for the same things everyone else lives for. We did not go in search of the King of Easter; he came and found us. This is our qualification for knowing him: we were not qualified. This is how God's blessing came to us through Abraham. This is how it can now flow through us—from our neighborhoods all the way to other nations.

Prayer

Father, just like you graciously called Abraham, you've called me to yourself. Abraham believed you, and it was counted to him as righteousness. I believe you too, Lord. I take a moment now to remember the sorrow of the days before the King of Easter came to find me [brief pause]. Thank you for calling me by name. You can take a normal worshiper of false gods, like me, and make them a blessing to the world. My King, make me a blessing. Amen.

DAY 8 | THURSDAY

READ JUDGES 2:6–23; 21:25

*In those days there was no king in Israel.
Everyone did what was right in his own eyes.*

Judges 21:25

Sometimes the behavior of God's people is almost embarrassing to read. The trouble wasn't so much that they didn't have a great king; God was their king, but they would not have him. Showing themselves not-so-far removed from the Garden of Eden, they wanted to do what seemed right to themselves. This is the storyline of the world. This is the story of our lives. We are not so removed from the people of the Book of Judges. Our kingdoms may be little—our homes, our cars, our phones, our thoughts—but we are often looking for another king to rule them. And often we make ourselves that king.

Prayer

Father, I often fail to trust in you with all my heart. Instead, I lean on my own understanding. I fail to submit my ways to you, when you would be delighted to clear a path before me. I have been wise in my own eyes and missed out on the healing and nourishment of your kingship. I recognize this isn't just the way of the world, but it's also my way of doing things. My King, pour out your mercy on me today. Amen.

DAY 9 | FRIDAY

READ 2 CHRONICLES 7:1–22

*If people who are called by my name humble themselves,
and pray and seek my face and turn from their wicked ways,
then I will hear from heaven and will forgive their sin
and heal their land.*

2 Chronicles 7:14

It's easy for us to point our fingers at others and blame them for the state of the world. When we hear a news story about violence in our city or in another country, our natural inclination is to assign guilt and distance ourselves from the perpetrators. But God calls his people to own their part in the mess. Here in 2 Chronicles, he is reminding Solomon that the people will inevitably go astray, but also that he has made a way for them to be brought back. When we are proud and prayerless, our communion with God suffers, and our neighbors are left in desperate situations. But when we are humble and cry out to him, when we lament our violent world, God brings healing to us and extends healing through us.

Fasting & Prayer

Each Friday during Lent we invite you to fast, to literally hunger with longing for the hope of Easter to bless the nations. See the Fasting Guide in the front of this devotional for helpful details. Begin the day by meditating on God's promise from 2 Chronicles 7:14. During a fasted meal time, look through some of today's news headlines. Resist the urge to assign guilt and distance yourself, and instead lament the circumstances and allow your heart to cry out to God in intercession. When you end the fast with a meal, rejoice in the God who promises to hear, forgive, and heal.

DAY 10 | SATURDAY

READ JOSHUA 2:1–24

And as soon as we heard it, our hearts melted, and there was no spirit left in any man because of you, for the Lord your God, he is God in the heavens above and on the earth beneath.

Joshua 2:11

The people of Jericho had heard of God's glory and his destruction of Egypt, but it only made their hearts harder. Rahab, on the other hand, her heart melted in the best of ways. She feared God and chose to follow him at great risk. It may even be that God sent his spies not so much to scope out the land, but to rescue this one precious believer and her family. Not only does the author parallel her with Joshua in chapter 1, but he also shows how Rahab permanently joins God's people (see Joshua 6:25). More than that, we eventually see her listed as one of the grandmothers of Jesus himself (see Matthew 1:5). You see, even during the time of Joshua, God was making himself known to the nations, and rescuing the most unlikely people.

Prayer

Father, you reveal yourself to those who do not ask for you. You are found by those who do not seek you. All day long you hold out your hands to obstinate people who walk in their own ways, pursuing their own crooked schemes. Thank you for purchasing us with the life of your Son. As one person among those faraway nations, like Rahab, I thank you for revealing yourself to me. You are God in heaven above and on the earth below. During these Lenten days, let my heart melt before you in the best of ways. Amen.

SUNDAY

Sundays during Lent are not counted as part of the forty days because they are traditionally reserved for public worship. In order to provide space to focus on gathering with your local church, this book does not include a Sunday devotional. However, we do encourage you to read Scripture, pray, and practice other spiritual disciples as you see fit. The devotional will continue on Monday.

DAY 11 | MONDAY

READ 1 KINGS 4:29–34, ECCLESIASTES 1:12–18

*I have seen everything that is done under the sun,
and behold, all is vanity and a striving after wind.
What is crooked cannot be made straight,
and what is lacking cannot be counted.*

Ecclesiastes 1:14–15

The beginning of Solomon's reign in Israel appeared to be what the world had been waiting for. He was trending as the wisest man around. Yet by the end of his rule, though he had nearly gained the world, he had also nearly forfeited his soul. "My people are destroyed from a lack of knowledge," God would later say in Hosea 4:6—not a lack of information, but a lack of transformation. They didn't know the God who could straighten what was crooked.

Western culture places a tremendously high value on knowledge. We give credibility to those who write books, have degrees, and sound like they know what they're talking about. This may be why we Westerners carry a sense of superiority toward those of non-Western culture and language. Yet the Lord looks upon the heart, and he invites us to see with his eyes. He wants to straighten us out.

Prayer

Father, fearing you is the beginning of true knowledge. Yet too often I see information, not transformation, as the goal. Lord, I remind myself that your wisdom was fully on display in your Son, Jesus. Though he is foolishness to the world, he is wisdom to me. Just as the nations marveled at the wisdom of Solomon, I pray the nations would wonder at the wisdom of Christ. As I journey with him to the cross in this season, I long not simply to know *about* him, but to know him. Amen.

DAY 12 | TUESDAY

READ 2 CHRONICLES 6:12–42

*Hear from heaven your dwelling place and do
according to all for which the foreigner calls to you,
in order that all the peoples of the earth may know your name and
fear you, as do your people Israel, and that they may know
that this house that I have built is called by your name.*

2 Chronicles 6:33

In this passage, King Solomon offers a prayer of dedication over the temple, the epicenter of God's glory on the earth at that time. We can only imagine what a wonder this was for the people of Israel. Surely, no people group has ever had more temptation to be ethnocentristic! But amazingly, within his prayer Solomon intercedes on behalf of foreigners, and he exudes the desire that all the peoples of the earth may know the one true God. This may seem like a strange aside in the flow of the prayer, but not if you know God's heart. This is why we don't just stop at introspection during Lent. As we encounter afresh God's willingness to dwell with sinners like us, it carries our prayers aside, for the sake of other foreigners too.

Prayer

Father, as you have called me to be hospitable to strangers, I make room for them today in my prayer. [Let the Lord bring a name or face to mind.] Let my life be a temple where others can encounter you. Too often I hoard your blessing; forgive me, Lord. Receive and perfect this little prayer like you did Solomon's. May I live for your unshakeable kingdom and be happy to welcome others into it. Amen.

DAY 13 | WEDNESDAY

READ PSALM 2

*Ask of me, and I will make the nations your heritage,
and the ends of the earth your possession.
You shall break them with a rod of iron and
dash them in pieces like a potter's vessel.*

Psalm 2:8–9

This psalm casts a broad light on God's plan for the nations. Though he is a refuge for all people, those who reject him will rage against him. So God has set up his Son as King and will soon bring judgment to those who don't pay homage to him alone. God's heart for the world doesn't come as a flimsy invitation; it's a warning for the day he will rule with a rod of iron and end the nations' raging by dashing them to pieces in his just judgment. If this were not true, then there would be no need for Easter. But because Easter has come, we know that God "has fixed a day on which he will judge the world in righteousness by a man whom he has appointed; and of this he has given assurance to all by raising him from the dead" (Acts 17:31).

Prayer

Father, those who do not believe you stand condemned already. There is only one name under heaven given among men by which we must be saved. I, too, once raged against you in my ignorance. But you have graciously opened my eyes and turned me from dark to light, and from the power of Satan to God. I thank you and I cry out for your mercy on behalf of those who continue to rage against you. Amen.

DAY 14 | THURSDAY

READ PSALM 67

May God be gracious to us and bless us and make his face to shine upon us, that your way may be known on earth, your saving power among all nations.

Psalm 67:1–2

When God's love meets us in our desperation, it leads to a certain kind of response. Grace changes us. This has always been God's design for his people: filling them with himself so that others know who he is, what he's like, and how to encounter him. The missionary God is not one who makes people go live in another country as penance for partying too hard in college; instead, God lavishes us with his kindness until we say, "May the peoples praise you, O God, may all the peoples praise you!"

Prayer

Father, as I am still before you, remind me how your love first met me in my desperation [pause], Now, from a grateful heart I pray: be gracious to me and bless me. Make your face shine upon me, so that your ways may be known on earth, your salvation among all peoples. May all the peoples praise you! May the nations be glad and sing for joy, for you rule the peoples with equity and guide the nations of the earth. Amen.

DAY 15 | FRIDAY

READ PSALM 78

*In spite of all this, they still sinned;
despite his wonders, they did not believe.*

Psalm 78:32

Over and over God's Old Testament people rebelled against him, were judged severely, and came crawling back. God's gracious discipline was never enough to keep them from wandering. They needed someone to take the full measure of his wrath and seal them with his Spirit. On this side of the cross, we know that someone was Christ, but for God's people in the Old Testament, this cycle of judgment-repentance-restoration was the best they could hope for until the Messiah would come. It was even worse for the nations outside of Israel because they didn't even know this path to restoration existed. They had nothing in their future but the seemingly endless consequences of living in a fallen world.

Fasting & Prayer

Each Friday during Lent we invite you to fast, to literally hunger with longing for the hope of Easter to bless the nations. See the Fasting Guide in the front of this devotional for helpful details. Begin the day by imagining yourself in the shoes of someone before the coming of Christ. During a fasted meal time, take a walk and pray for the people you see, many of whom will be trapped in a cycle of death. End the fast with a meal and have a spirit of rejoicing in the God who saves from both sin and its power.

DAY 16 | SATURDAY

READ PSALM 106

Both we and our fathers have sinned; we have committed iniquity; we have done wickedness.

Psalm 106:6

Rather than being a bright beacon of God's glory among the nations, Israel often joined in their idolatry. They were a hard-hearted people, and in Psalm 106, the psalmist unabashedly admits it. Not only does he give example after example of failure, but he also includes himself among the rebels. It's not that he's wallowing; he's marveling. Marveling at the God of steadfast love.

We can only arrive at Easter marveling when along the way we've admitted our own hard-heartedness. God has already given Jesus the nations as an inheritance and possession, and in that authority Jesus commands us to go and make disciples of all nations. Yet we are often filled with hesitations when it comes to crossing cultures, even in our own neighborhoods. Lent is a chance for us to acknowledge this and see the God of steadfast love still coming after us.

Prayer

Father, the earth is yours and everything in it. You see my hesitation toward engaging people who are different from me. You see how I join in idolatry rather than showing others the way out of it. Forgive me according to your steadfast love. Encourage me today with the confidence that Christ is ruling over the whole world and sending me to claim what already belongs to him. Fill my mouth and open their hearts, that the King of glory may come in. Amen.

SUNDAY

Sundays during Lent are not counted as part of the forty days because they are traditionally reserved for public worship. In order to provide space to focus on gathering with your local church, this book does not include a Sunday devotional. However, we do encourage you to read Scripture, pray, and practice other spiritual disciples as you see fit. The devotional will continue on Monday.

DAY 17 | MONDAY

READ ISAIAH 49:1–7

*It is too light a thing that you should be my servant
to raise up the tribes of Jacob and to bring back
the preserved of Israel; I will make you as a light for the nations,
that my salvation may reach to the end of the earth.*

Isaiah 49:6

Here Isaiah prophesies of a servant unlike any who has come before. God is speaking through his prophet to describe Israel's Messiah as one who will finally complete the original mission to fill the earth with God's glory. This means his salvation will extend well beyond the ethnic and geographic boundaries of Israel. It will reach into all nations.

This is likely good news for you in the same way! For you, too, are probably a Gentile in a dark land. It's always tempting, especially for Westerners, to view our own land as the epicenter of Christianity, to believe that God's mission is, for example, "from the West to the rest." But as we wander through these forty days toward the promised land of Easter, it's good to sit alone and be silent and lay our faces in the dust (see Lamentations 3:25–33). We have been desperate recipients. Let us also be grateful ones.

Prayer

Father, I see the world through the lens of my own culture. I sometimes forget that I was once not among your chosen people; instead, I was dead in my trespasses and sins, like a dry, fruitless branch. Yet by your grace you grafted me into your people. Thank you! Remind me today of the amazing mystery now revealed even to the ends of the earth: Christ in us, the hope of glory. Amen

DAY 18 | TUESDAY

READ ISAIAH 52:13–53:12

He was despised and rejected by men,
a man of sorrows and acquainted with grief;
and as one from whom men hide their faces
he was despised, and we esteemed him not.

Isaiah 53:3

The journey of the world to this point in the story has been one of suffering and tragedy. How desperately we needed a messianic man of sorrows, one who would identify with our griefs in every way. That world that clamored for sword-wielding heroes would not understand a crucified Christ. Today's world of religious extremism, economic jockeying, and political scheming still doesn't understand him. To follow the man of sorrows into this world is to be a person of sorrows as well. As we lament our world's blood-soaked lust for power, and we grieve with those harmed by it, we will be misunderstood as well. What good company we find ourselves in!

Prayer

Father, thank you for sending your Son as a suffering servant. Thank you that he took my pain and bore my sorrow, was pierced for my transgressions and crushed for my iniquities. Thank you that he will justify many and sprinkle many nations. I pray for those today who put their hope in sword-wielding heroes. May their disappointment in such men prepare their hearts for the glory of the One who gave himself for us. Amen.

DAY 19 | WEDNESDAY

READ ISAIAH 61

*For as the earth brings forth its sprouts,
and as a garden causes what is sown in it to sprout up,
so the Lord God will cause righteousness and praise
to sprout up before all the nations.*

Isaiah 61:11

Rarely does a moment go by in the Scriptures when God does not in some way express his heart for all nations. When discussing global missions, many people turn immediately to the New Testament and the Great Commission. But our entire foundation for understanding God's mission comes from the Old Testament. His glorious, loving, pursuing character is on display long before the Incarnation, and this mission he calls us into is not a ministry for only part of the church to participate in. It flows from our very identity as sons and daughters of the sending God.

Lent is a time for sowing. We are eager for righteousness and praise to sprout up before all nations. But first we sow in tears—longing, waiting, wondering if we will ever reap a harvest (see Psalm 126). Join in the weeping, that you may join in the reaping.

Prayer

Father, I delight greatly in you. My soul rejoices because you are my God. You have clothed me with garments of salvation and given me a robe of righteousness. Lord, as you advance your kingdom among all nations, show me how I can participate with you. I want to sow, even if it's hard. I believe one day I will reap with you, if I do not lose heart. Amen.

DAY 20 | THURSDAY

READ JONAH 3:6–4:11

When God saw what they did, how they turned from their evil way, God relented of the disaster that he had said he would do to them, and he did not do it. But it displeased Jonah exceedingly, and he was angry.

Jonah 3:10–4:1

Let's be honest: Jonah's attitude is so pitiful it's almost funny. Yet when we deeply consider the circumstances, the story has a profound message for us. God's compassion always falls on those who don't deserve it, which is good news—until it's poured out upon someone we can't stand. Words can't describe how vile the Assyrians had been to other nations, especially Israel. It was tortuous for Jonah to watch them receive mercy. No wonder he was angry enough to die.

Do you get uncomfortable thinking about certain people receiving the mercy of God? Is it a politician, criminal, or personal enemy? Is there a nation or people group that tends to rub you the wrong way? Take a moment to consider this and confess it to your merciful Father.

Prayer

Father, you are gracious and compassionate, slow to anger and rich in love. Thank you for your mercy toward those who don't deserve it. I certainly didn't deserve it, and I still don't. Forgive me for the limitations I want to place on your grace. Even if no one comes to mind that I would struggle to welcome into your family, please search me, O God, and know my heart. Test me and know my anxious thoughts. See if there is any displeasing way in me, and lead me in the way of your endless grace. Amen.

DAY 21 | FRIDAY

READ EZEKIEL 36:16–38

*And I will give you a new heart,
and a new spirit I will put within you.
And I will remove the heart of stone from your flesh
and give you a heart of flesh. And I will put my Spirit within you . . .*

Ezekiel 36:26–27

The prophet Ezekiel passes on harsh words from the Lord to the exiled people of Israel. His frustration is evident: they have profaned his name among the nations. But God promises to advance the mission himself and to accomplish it by putting his Spirit in his people. Even after Jesus's resurrection and the coming of the Holy Spirit, God's people have not always been quick to join him in his mission to the world. However, God has shown himself faithful to use his people to continue to accomplish his mission. Though our hearts and flesh are weak, though we are fearful and at times falter in our faithfulness, God is gracious to accomplish his redemption mission through his people, the church.

Fasting & Prayer

Each Friday during Lent we invite you to fast, to literally hunger with longing for the hope of Easter to bless the nations. See the Fasting Guide in the front of this devotional for helpful details. Begin the day by remembering how impossible it was to please God before you were given a new heart through the death and resurrection of Jesus. During a fasted meal time, go to Operation World (operationworld.org) and follow the prayer prompts for the day. Ask God to carry out his plan to bring the gospel to this region of the world. When you end your fast with a meal, rejoice in the Spirit who has been poured into your heart and is actively at work among the people you prayed for.

DAY 22 | SATURDAY

READ HABAKKUK 2

For the earth will be filled with the knowledge of the glory of the Lord as the waters cover the sea.

Habakkuk 2:14

We are a people who squirm and fret at life's what-ifs. Though we've seen the Father in the face of Jesus Christ, we still struggle each day to trust his promises. Yet he is faithful, not only in the smallest of life's details but also in the grandest of his plans. When it comes to God's plan for the whole world, we can know without a doubt that God will fill the earth with the knowledge of his glory as the waters cover the sea. We can also take comfort in the truth that "the Lord is in his holy temple" and invites the whole earth—every nation and people—to come and be silent in his presence (Habakkuk 2:20).

Prayer

Father, you sit enthroned above the circle of the earth. You stretch out the heavens like a canopy. You determine the number of stars in the sky and call them each by name. Surely, the nations are like a drop in a bucket. Their hatred and rage against the things of God are no threat to you, for you have power over all things. Yet, Romans 5 tells us that even while we were living in sin, living in opposition to you, you sent your Son to die so that we might live. His death and resurrection provide a path of life for all nations. You promise to cover the whole world with the knowledge of your glory. I sit silently before you in anticipation of seeing your promise fulfilled. Amen.

SUNDAY

Sundays during Lent are not counted as part of the forty days because they are traditionally reserved for public worship. In order to provide space to focus on gathering with your local church, this book does not include a Sunday devotional. However, we do encourage you to read Scripture, pray, and practice other spiritual disciples as you see fit. The devotional will continue on Monday.

DAY 23 | MONDAY

READ MALACHI 1:6–14

Cursed be the cheat who has a male in his flock, and vows it, and yet sacrifices to the Lord what is blemished. For I am a great King, says the Lord of hosts, and my name will be feared among the nations.

Malachi 1:14

God spared himself no expense in accomplishing our salvation, and he'll spare us no expense in shaping us into his image. He deserves and demands the best we have to offer so that he might be glorified among the nations. But rather than offering ourselves as living sacrifices, we withhold from God. Like the people addressed in Malachi, we pick and choose what we are willing to give to God and what we will withhold. Too often, instead of living on mission by surrendering our desires for our homes, neighborhoods, classrooms, and cubicles, we hold them tightly in fear and refusal. For most people, serving cross-culturally is definitely off-limits. "What a burden!" our hearts cry. Yet, when we reflect on the beauty of Jesus being seen and known "from the rising of the sun to its setting" (Psalm 113:3), we should open our grip on these things and offer them willingly to the Lord. Will you?

Prayer

Father, in view of your mercies, I desire to present myself to you as a living sacrifice, holy and pleasing. I want to lay my gifts, talents, resources—even my weaknesses—before you and ask you to use me to make your name great in my home, neighborhood, classroom, cubicle, and even among the nations. On this pilgrim road to Easter, I offer myself to you in the midst of my hesitations, knowing I can always draw near with confidence to your throne of grace. Amen.

DAY 24 | TUESDAY

READ LUKE 2:22–38

*... For my eyes have seen your salvation
that you have prepared in the presence of all peoples,
a light for revelation to the Gentiles,
and for glory to your people Israel.*

Luke 2:30–32

The long-awaited Savior had finally come, born of a virgin as the sinless Son of God. Before he uttered more than a squeal, a faithful man named Simeon who had been longing for his arrival scooped him up and announced the fulfillment of what the prophets had long foretold: a Savior had come to redeem a broken and lost people. The child that Simeon held in his hands had come for the salvation of all peoples. The coming of the Messiah was the fulfillment of promises God made to the nation of Israel, and to all nations. Once again, God was proving himself faithful.

Prayer

Father, as someone from the ends of the earth, I thank you so much that I can say "For unto us a child is born, unto us a son is given." He is my Wonderful Counselor, my Mighty God, my Everlasting Father, my Prince of Peace. Thank you for Immanuel, "God with us." For my eyes have seen your salvation, which you have prepared in the sight of all nations. Thank you, God, for your promises fulfilled. Amen.

DAY 25 | WEDNESDAY

READ JOHN 4:4–42

They said to the woman, "It is no longer because of what you said that we believe, for we have heard for ourselves, and we know that this is indeed the Savior of the world."

John 4:42

Here, Jesus, a Jewish man, smashes cultural norms by engaging a Samaritan woman. Most Jews would have considered her an outcast from society and unworthy of their time or attention, yet in his kindness, Jesus takes time to come to her, have a conversation with her, and reveal himself as the promised Messiah. By graciously receiving her and her entire village, Jesus also turns the apostles' thinking upside down. Jesus shows his disciples that he came to redeem all people, even the peoples beyond Jerusalem and Judea. And as we'll see, they were often more ready to receive him than the people of Israel.

Prayer

Father, you did not send your Son to call the healthy, but the sick; not the respectable, but the outcast. Thank you that Jesus came to seek and to save the lost, like me. Thank you for your willingness to cross cultural boundaries, no matter what it cost you. Forgive me for assuming I know who is ready to receive you and who isn't. Help me to have a broken and contrite spirit, that I may be sensitive to those who are broken, poor, sick, and ready for a Savior. Jesus, give me the heart you had when you moved toward the Samaritan woman with compassion. Amen.

DAY 26 | THURSDAY

READ LUKE 4:14–30

When they heard these things, all in the synagogue were filled with wrath. And they rose up and drove him out of the town and brought him to the brow of the hill on which their town was built, so that they could throw him down the cliff.

Luke 4:28–29

Jesus opens his public ministry with a prophetic word that draws nothing but fury from those in his hometown. As Jesus is teaching in the synagogue in Nazareth, he reminds the Jewish audience of two Old Testament instances in which God's grace was extended to Gentiles rather than Jews. As you may know, the tension between Jews and Gentiles was great, and this prophecy did not land well on his hearers. The implication of Jesus's teaching from the Scriptures is that the Lord's favor had fallen upon the Gentiles whose hearts were open and willing, while the Jews would miss out because their hearts were hard. We see this reality play out through much of the New Testament. This story in Luke 4 is a warning to us to guard ourselves against hoarding God's grace and a reminder that God often works among the people we least expect. Praise God for his grace that knows no bounds.

Prayer

Father, thank you for sending your Son to proclaim good news to the poor, freedom for the captives, and recovery of sight for the blind. Thank you that he was filled with both grace and truth, speaking hard things that we needed to hear. Lord, continue to give me a heart of grace that genuinely rejoices at any sign of your kingdom and remembers the joy of making room for others. Amen.

DAY 27 | FRIDAY

READ MARK 11:1–19

*. . . he overturned the tables of the money-changers
. . . saying to them, "Is it not written,
'My house shall be called a house of prayer for all the nations'?
But you have made it a den of robbers."*

Mark 11:15b, 17

We are all prone to turning things to our own advantage. Our hearts are deceptive and tend toward self-centeredness and self-gain. Like the money changers in this story, we can even see the people of God and the local churches we gather with as places of competition, consumerism, and self-focus. Even without knowing it, our sinful hearts cause us to ask, "How can others meet my needs?" or "How can the church fulfill all my expectations?" Yet, God's desire is that we would live, serve, and abide with God's people in such a way that we would think of ourselves last, that we would sacrifice for the sake of others in the church. This kind of selfless living is pleasing to the Lord.

Fasting & Prayer

Each Friday during Lent we invite you to fast, to literally hunger with longing for the hope of Easter to bless the nations. See the Fasting Guide in the front of this devotional for helpful details. Begin the day by asking God to reveal your tendency to use the church to your own advantage. During a fasted meal time, pray for the hearts of your fellow church members, that they would be prepared for Easter, and that this preparation would move them toward greater eagerness to participate in God's mission. When the fast ends with a meal, rejoice in the God who delights to give rather than receive.

DAY 28 | SATURDAY

READ JOHN 10:1–16; 17:20–23

*And I have other sheep that are not of this fold.
I must bring them also, and they will listen to my voice.
So there will be one flock, one shepherd.*

John 10:16

The theme of Jesus's concern for more than just the Jews reached its peak at the conclusion of his life and ministry. Jesus's mission of redemption was and is centered on all peoples of the earth. He thought of them, talked about them, and prayed for them. This is more than an abstract fact for us, because we are the beneficiaries of Jesus's work. Jesus was thinking of *us*, talking about *us*, and praying for *us* on his way to the cross. When Jesus said, "I have other sheep that are not of this fold. I must bring them also, and they will listen to my voice," he was referring to us, his church. Jesus's love for us and pursuit of us was and is undeniable. Because the Triune God now lives in us through the power of the Holy Spirit, it makes sense that we also would think of, talk about, and pray for the nations of the earth. As we grow in closeness to and affection for Jesus, our love and concern for the nations grows as well.

Prayer

Father, thank you for your Son who is at your right hand even as I pray, interceding for me. Thank you that he thought of me, talked about me, and prayed for me. Yet I recognize it was not only for me, but for all of his lost sheep scattered throughout the earth. I ask that you would draw the nations to Christ just as you drew me to yourself. May the world know you as I know you: as a kind and loving Father. Amen.

SUNDAY

Sundays during Lent are not counted as part of the forty days because they are traditionally reserved for public worship. In order to provide space to focus on gathering with your local church, this book does not include a Sunday devotional. However, we do encourage you to read Scripture, pray, and practice other spiritual disciples as you see fit. The devotional will continue on Monday.

DAY 29 | MONDAY

READ MATTHEW 24:1–14

And this gospel of the kingdom will be proclaimed throughout the whole world as a testimony to all nations, and then the end will come.

Matthew 24:14

In Matthew 24, Jesus lays out some significant guarantees in his global mission: the nations will rage, the church will suffer, and the gospel will advance. Some have made this passage into a formula, saying that as soon as we preach the gospel to every nation, Jesus will automatically return. But this interpretation demonstrates a misunderstanding of the passage. Jesus's return is not dependent on us, and he makes it clear that no one knows the day or hour of his coming (Matthew 24:36). All we know is that God will advance his good news through his people, and when the time is right, Jesus will return in all his glory. This truth has the power to fill us with confidence, boldness, and a willingness to sacrifice.

This Lenten season of waiting on Easter is an excellent training ground for learning to wait more desperately for Jesus's second coming. As we do this with eager anticipation, may we live our lives on mission for others so that they may experience his forgiveness, goodness, and eternal fellowship.

Prayer

Father, you have guaranteed that your mission will succeed. This is my confidence before you, that if I ask anything according to your will, you hear me. And if you hear me, I know I have whatever I asked of you. Fill me now with confidence in your global mission so I have words to fearlessly make known the mystery of the gospel to others. Amen.

DAY 30 | TUESDAY

READ JOHN 10:17–18; 19:16–30

*No one takes it from me,
but I lay it down of my own accord.
I have authority to lay it down,
and I have authority to take it up again . . .*

John 10:18

In the introduction we wrote that this was the mountaintop of human history, the defining event of the Christian life. Jesus, the Son of God, laid down his life and died. He did so willingly, in obedience to his Father, so that you and I could be restored back to God and have eternal fellowship with him. Jesus completed what Isaiah had foretold so long ago, that the Messiah would be "pierced for our transgressions . . . crushed for our iniquities" (Isaiah 53:5). Jesus kept the law we couldn't keep. Jesus took on the wrath of God for the sins of the world, a weight we couldn't bear. Jesus became our atoning sacrifice and brought us back into a loving relationship with God.

This gospel truth is both cosmic and personal. His death and resurrection shook the foundations of the earth; it was the climax of human history. But it's also a part of your personal story. Jesus died and rose again for *you*. As you think about this radical truth, how does Jesus's sacrifice stir your heart? How does it move you to worship?

Prayer

Father, your Word says, "cursed is everyone who is hanged on a tree" (Galatians 3:13). Thank you for sending Christ to redeem me from the curse of the law by becoming a curse for me. Thank you that his cosmic work is applied to me personally. Lord, give me the grace I need to cling to this gospel and to find hope in you when life seems hopeless and my strength fails. Amen.

DAY 31 | WEDNESDAY

READ JOHN 20:1–23

*Jesus said to them again,
"Peace be with you. As the Father has sent me,
even so I am sending you."*

John 20:21

A core foundational truth in Scripture is that everything begins with God, and that includes mission. Out of the overflow of his perfect, eternal communion as Father, Son, and Spirit, God initiated a chain reaction of sending. Though we might think that his sending culminated in the Incarnation, God is continuing a progression of redemptive sending to this day. Just as Jesus was sent out on mission from the Father, and the Spirit was sent into the world from the Father and Son, the church is now sent out on mission by the Triune God. As his children, we are shaped and commissioned to continue his sending work by making disciples of all nations.

Our mission is more than mere activity—it's an identity we've been given. When the Spirit draws us to himself and we repent and believe, we're not only given salvation, but our very identity is changed as well. To follow Jesus means that we make Jesus's name and glory known to others because of what he has done for us. It's a love that we can't keep to ourselves; we have to give it away.

Prayer

Father, knowing what it means to love and follow you, I want to invite others into our family. It is not fear, guilt, or shame that compels me to live this life, but the love of Jesus, the one who died for me and was raised again. Thank you for making peace between us through your Son's sacrifice. Help me to extend that peace to others, not as a duty, but as part of who I am. Amen.

DAY 32 | THURSDAY

READ MATTHEW 28

And Jesus came and said to them, "All authority in heaven and on earth has been given to me. Go therefore and make disciples of all nations . . ."

Matthew 28:18–19

This is the passage we've all been waiting for, right? Matthew 28:18–20 is the clearest and most robust picture of the Great Commission. God's people are called to move out toward others, make the gospel known, disciple, baptize, and continue teaching all that Jesus has commanded. Jesus's last word to his followers before ascending is clear: go and make disciples of all nations.

Friends, this is a beautiful and weighty command from Jesus, and if we're honest with ourselves, this command can seem too hard at times. How can we live in this broken world, full of life and responsibilities, and still be faithful to carry out his Great Commission? It just feels impossible. And maybe that's the key to it all, that when we seek to live on mission in our own strength, it's not possible. Yet, the last words of Jesus move this commission from an impossible command to a joyful way of life. In verse 20, Jesus says, "And behold, I am with you always, to the end of the age."

Did you see that? Jesus promises to be with us as we live on mission him. Sharing Jesus with others and making new disciples is possible and life-giving because the Creator and Sustainer of the world is with us. His presence makes the mission possible. More than that, it moves us from despair to joyful obedience.

Prayer

Father, in your wisdom you've seen fit to use your broken and limited church to make the glories of Jesus known to a watching world. We are your people and your instrument of redemption in the world around us. But I confess that I'm afraid and feel so insufficient for the mission you've called me to. In your kindness, give me the courage to declare the goodness of your grace to others and invite people to experience you, knowing that you are with me. You promise to strengthen me and be ever-present. May these truths hold me fast. Amen.

DAY 33 | FRIDAY

READ ACTS 1:6–11

But you will receive power when the Holy Spirit has come upon you, and you will be my witnesses in Jerusalem and in all Judea and Samaria, and to the end of the earth.

Acts 1:8

Moments before Jesus ascended into heaven to be with the Father, he reminded his disciples the promised Holy Spirit would come. He would work in them to accomplish all that Jesus had entrusted to the church, namely, to make him known near and far.

Acts 1:8 is instructive for Christians today as well. The Spirit is the power at work in us that allows us to live on mission to the world around us. It is the Holy Spirit, his indwelling presence in our lives, who allows us to share Jesus, make disciples, and even plant new churches in places near us, around us, and far from us. Once again we are reminded that the mission God has given to his church is not dependent on our strength or strategies or skill, but on the power of the Holy Spirit at work in our lives.

Fasting & Prayer

Each Friday during Lent we invite you to fast, to literally hunger with longing for the hope of Easter to bless the nations. See the Fasting Guide in the front of this devotional for helpful details. Begin the day by meditating on how the Holy Spirit comes to empower you as a witness. During a fasted meal time, pray that God would lead you to people he has prepared to receive the gospel, and that he would give you the boldness to speak. Confess honestly to your loving Father the things that hold you back from such confidence. When you end the fast with a meal, rejoice in the power of the Holy Spirit who makes you a witness.

DAY 34 | SATURDAY

READ ACTS 2:1–41

And suddenly there came from heaven a sound like a mighty rushing wind, and it filled the entire house where they were sitting. And divided tongues as of fire appeared to them and rested on each one of them.

Acts 2:2–3

Remember the story of the tower of Babel from Genesis 11? There, God judged the people for their sins by dispersing them around the earth and giving them separate languages. From that event, people groups, nations, cultures, and languages began to develop. Now fast-forward thousands of years to the coming of the Holy Spirit in Acts 2. This story is like a bookend to Babel. Notice that the Spirit arrives as "tongues of fire," allowing the apostles to preach the gospel in the unique languages of different people groups gathered in Jerusalem.

In a way, with the coming of the Holy Spirit at Pentecost, we see a reversal of what happened at Babel. Not that the distinction of ethnicities, languages, or cultures ends—these are beautiful reflections of God's diverse people (see Revelation 7:9–12). Rather, what we see at Pentecost is the gospel bringing life and restoration to a people in need of a Savior. Once again, we see the mercy of God on display in his work of redemption.

Prayer

Father, when you send forth your Spirit, your people are made new, and you renew the face of the earth. I want to be renewed in these forty days. Thank you for establishing your church as a people made up of all nations. Through the church, your manifold wisdom is put on display. May you be glorified in your church and in Christ Jesus forever and ever. Amen.

SUNDAY

Sundays during Lent are not counted as part of the forty days because they are traditionally reserved for public worship. In order to provide space to focus on gathering with your local church, this book does not include a Sunday devotional. However, we do encourage you to read Scripture, pray, and practice other spiritual disciples as you see fit. The devotional will continue on Monday.

DAY 35 | MONDAY

READ ACTS 10

While Peter was still saying these things, the Holy Spirit fell on all who heard the word. And the believers from among the circumcised who had come with Peter were amazed, because the gift of the Holy Spirit was poured out even on the Gentiles.

Acts 10:44–45

It may seem like just another turn in the story, but this is the official entrance of the Gentiles into the family of God. The Old Testament, along with the Gospels, makes it clear that the coming of the Messiah was for the Gentiles as well as the Jews, but it's in the story of Peter and Cornelius that the reality of this promise hits home. The Messiah is for everyone! What may be a clear and simple truth for us was a radical unfolding of God's love for the early church. Hostility between Jews and Gentiles was historic and ran deep, but the gospel brings reconciliation, not only between God and man, but also between man and man.

Among God's people, there is no longer Jew or Gentile, slave or free, male or female, for all are one in Christ Jesus (Galatians 3:28–29). Ephesians 2:14 makes it clear: ". . . [Jesus] himself is our peace, who has made us both one and has broken down in his flesh the dividing wall of hostility." The gospel is both vertical, bringing us back to God, and horizontal, breaking down walls of hostility between peoples, nations, and languages.

Prayer

Father, who is a God like you, who pardons sin and forgives transgression? You do not stay angry forever, but delight to show mercy. Through your grace, you draw us to yourself through the work of your Son and then move us out toward one another. Too often I underestimate your love for me and your ability to bring wholeness to my broken world. Thank you for your love that goes beyond my understanding. Amen.

DAY 36 | TUESDAY

READ ACTS 11:19–26; 13:1–4

While they were worshiping the Lord and fasting, the Holy Spirit said, "Set apart for me Barnabas and Saul for the work to which I have called them." Then after fasting and praying they laid their hands on them and sent them off.

Acts 13:2–3

The church at Antioch was not only the first place believers were called Christians, but it was also the first church to actively display its sentness. The church at Antioch was a multicultural church, with Jewish and Gentile believers gathered from the nations, committed to worshiping the Lord together. Through their commitment to worshiping and fasting, God called out Saul (Paul), Barnabas, and John Mark as cross-cultural missionaries from the local church.

This story is significant in the history of missions. God could have used the church in Jerusalem as the first church to intentionally send its people to the nations, but instead, God chose a new church plant, full of new believers, full of the nations, to send out to the nations. Beautiful!

Knowing the story of the church at Antioch and the way God chooses to use his faithful people, how could God use your local church to reach the nations of the earth?

Prayer

Father, your Son laid down his life for his bride, the church. One day she will be united to you fully and forever. But until that day, she is your hands and feet, used to proclaim the excellencies of you who called her out of darkness and into your marvelous light. Lord, help my local church to be faithful in the task of leaving our comfort to make you known to the nations of the earth. Give our pastors and leaders a vision for our role in your global mission. Help me to abandon comfort and move past distractions so that I can play a meaningful part in your kingdom work. Amen.

DAY 37 | WEDNESDAY

READ ROMANS 15:1–21

*And thus I make it my ambition to preach the gospel,
not where Christ has already been named,
lest I build on someone else's foundation.*

Romans 15:20

The apostle Paul was an amazing man of faith. Once a persecutor of the church, he then experienced persecution himself for declaring the gospel he formerly mocked. He was and is a model for us of a man fully committed to God, willing to sacrifice everything for the sake of knowing God and making him known to others.

It's tempting to make Paul the hero of his own story, but if we do, we miss the point. When we look at the life of Paul and other faithful men and women throughout church history, the amazing thing about their lives has nothing to do with *them* and everything to do with *God's grace at work in them*. Paul was able to stand under the hell of suffering and persecution, he was able to see fruit in ministry, he was able to finish well in this life, because the gospel he proclaimed was at work in him as well. Paul is a model for us because the gospel flowed both in him and through him.

This is why going to the unreached peoples and places of the earth was a passion for Paul. He wanted others to experience the same joy and life that he experienced daily. This is the great motivator for missionary work, a desire to experience Jesus and be with him where he is at work to shine his light into darkness. Lent has led us into darkness, but Easter's promise has enabled us to stay the path. The same will be true when we say, "Here am I! Send me" (Isaiah 6:8).

Prayer

Father, thank you for sending Paul to be a minister of Christ to the Gentiles. He proclaimed the gospel so that they might become an offering acceptable to you and sanctified by your Holy Spirit. By the same Spirit who lived in Paul, keep me from settling into what's comfortable and familiar. Move me to the edges of lostness and allow me to experience your grace as I give the gospel away to others. For I was made to be your salt and light. Amen.

DAY 38 | THURSDAY

READ 1 TIMOTHY 2:1–7

For there is one God, and there is one mediator between God and men, he man Christ Jesus, who gave himself as a ransom for all . . .

1 Timothy 2:5–6

The urgency of God's mission pivots on this reality: there is only one way back to God, and that is through the life, death, and resurrection of Jesus Christ (John 14:6). Missions only makes sense if people are lost and hellbound under the weight of their sin. Missions only makes sense if lost people are truly lost and in need of saving. Otherwise, if hell is not real or there is some other path to salvation, then why did Jesus have to die? As terrifying as the wrath of God and eternity apart from him is, these realities make the gospel even more glorious. They make the gospel good news. Jesus gave his life so that we could have life unending.

When you and I pray, we get to play an active role in seeing people come to faith in Jesus and find eternal life in him. Prayer is the fuel of global missions, and it's one of the primary ways God has given us to participate in it. When we pray, we are "fellow workers for the truth" (3 John 1:8), moving around the world, shaping people's lives and families, and changing whole communities. When we pray, we can have confidence that God is at work in the world and that he is impacting the people we pray for.

Prayer

Father, forgive me for my prayerlessness, especially toward those who are separated from Christ and without hope. You have made peace with me through the blood of your Son shed on the cross. Move my stubborn heart to care for those who don't know you. Move me to pray for their salvation, not out of guilt, but from the joy of knowing you. Amen.

DAY 39 | FRIDAY

READ ROMANS 9:1–5; 10:1–21

. . . I have great sorrow and unceasing anguish in my heart. For I could wish that I myself were accursed and cut off from Christ for the sake of my brothers, my kinsmen according to the flesh.

Romans 9:2–3

Good Friday is a day of contradiction. We call Good Friday "good," and indeed it is good. It's the day our Lord and Savior willingly died in our place so that we could have life in him. Yet, at the same time, it's the darkest day of the year, for it's the day that Jesus was nailed to the cross. It's the day we pause to remember and reflect on the great sacrifice God made so that we could be free from the curse of sin and death. Good Friday is a heavy day, but it is a good day as well. As you take time today to reflect on the cross and all that Jesus did for you, also take time to feel the weight of the lostness around you.

Paul was a man who knew contradiction. He committed his whole life to seeing Gentiles come to faith, yet he also felt a deep burden for his own people, the Jews. Paul grieved over them so much that, if he could have, he would have given up his own salvation for theirs. It's hard to comprehend this kind of love, but Paul was that broken over his people.

On this Good Friday, spend time with the Lord, asking him to give you the kind of brokenness for the lost that Paul experienced. Ask him to put specific people, places, and people groups on your mind and heart so that you might fall to your knees, weighed down with a burden for them, praying that these people may also know the beauty and pain of Good Friday and know our Savior who died for them.

Fasting & Prayer

Each Friday during Lent we invite you to fast, to literally hunger with longing for the hope of Easter to bless the nations. See the Fasting Guide in the front of this devotional for helpful details. The spirit of Paul's love and grief is informative for today's fast. Take time early in the day to meditate on a specific lost person or people. As you withhold from eating throughout the day, channel your hunger toward groans for their salvation. Allow yourself to sense their hopelessness and grieve their stubbornness. Conclude the fast with a meal and a spirit of rejoicing in the hope of God's great mercy.

DAY 40 | SATURDAY

READ REVELATION 7:9–12

After this I looked, and behold, a great multitude that no one could number, from every nation, from all tribes and peoples and languages, standing before the throne and before the Lamb, clothed in white robes, with palm branches in their hands, and crying out with a loud voice, "Salvation belongs to our God who sits on the throne, and to the Lamb!"

Revelation 7:9–10

Lent has been a journey of repentance and preparation for celebrating the life, death, and resurrection of Christ. We have laid our faces in the dirt, lamenting our own brokenness and the world's lostness. As Easter dawns tomorrow, it's good for our final meditation to be focused on the coming day when multitudes from every nation, tribe, people, and language will gather and celebrate together "the Lamb of God who takes away the sin of the world" (John 1:29).

Pause for a moment and consider this: Revelation 7 is both a picture and a promise. It's a picture of mission fulfillment. People from every language, tribe, nation, and tongue are standing in heaven before the Lamb of God, worshiping him for all eternity. This picture should help undergird our missions efforts, for it's a picture of missions fulfilled in eternal worship.

But Revelation 7 is also a promise, a promise that God will finish what he started. Yes, you and I play a meaningful role in seeing the nations of the earth come to faith in Jesus. However, the mission is not dependent on us; it is dependent on him. The picture in Revelation 7 of a multitude of nations worshiping Jesus is a promise that God, in his power and grace, will complete the mission he has given to us.

As you prepare your heart for Easter Sunday, take comfort in knowing that the nations *will* come and worship Jesus for all eternity. You are invited to play an active role in seeing them come to faith. But know that the mission of God will be completed by the God of the mission. He will finish what he started, and that, my friends, is good news!

Prayer

Father, thank you for your grace that has appeared and offered salvation to all people. Thank you that you have invited me into your mission to see the nations come to know you and worship you for all eternity. I also thank you that this Great Commission is not dependent on me, but on you and your faithfulness. You will finish what you started, and I take comfort in your promise fulfilled. Just as you sustained me through Lent and brought me renewed to Easter, I know you will continue to do the same until I finally see you face to face. Amen.

NEXT STEPS & RESOURCES

Below you will find resources and activities to help you grow in your walk with Jesus and your engagement in God's global mission. We've broken these resources into three sections to help you develop your knowledge, character, and skills.

We also deeply believe that a foundational aspect of growing as a follower of Jesus is faithfulness to a local church. If you're not a member of a local church, or currently find yourself disconnected from the body of Christ, we encourage you to find a Bible-teaching, gospel-centered, missions-hearted church in your area. Don't just attend sporadically, but jump into the life, community, and mission of the church. Just as Lent leads to Easter and onward to Pentecost (see the Book of Acts), the centrality of the local church is the most appropriate next step of involvement in God's mission.

HEAD
Books to help you grow in knowledge and understanding of God's global mission

Missionary biographies: *Hudson Taylor's Spiritual Secret* by Howard Taylor, *A Chance to Die: The Life and Legacy of Amy Carmichael* by Elisabeth Elliot, and *The Insanity of God* by Nik Ripken

Small group missions study: *You Are Sent: Finding Your Place in God's Global Missions* by Nathan Sloan

Deeper missions study: *Introducing World Missions: A Biblical, Historical, and Practical Guide* by Moreau, Corwin, and McGee

HEART
Tools and resources to help shape and refine your passion for God and his mission

Pray: Make it a habit to pray for the nations once a day. Build it into your devotional time, pray a short prayer before bed, or adopt a people group or missionary and pray for them during a family meal. Creating a simple prayer habit can be a significant step in growing your missions engagement. Consider downloading the Operation World app (operationworld.org) and using it as a daily prayer resource.

Read: Consider reading a book focused on cultivating a deeper abiding life with God, such as *Possibility of Prayer* by John Starke, *An Unhurried Life* by Alan Fadling, or *Gentle and Lowly* by Dane Ortland.

HANDS
Practical steps toward growth and deeper service

Eat: Find an international restaurant in your area that is owned and operated by internationals. Go there often as a family or a small group. Get to know the owners and workers of the restaurant. Consider inviting them to your home for a meal, and share the love of Jesus with them.

Learn and apply: Pick up a copy of *Tradecraft: For the Church on Mission*, read through the nine missional skills, and start applying them in your everyday life. Even better, read it in community with others.

Take your next step: Talk with the leaders of your church about your growing passion for global missions. Ask about opportunities to be sent out and how you can start growing and learning more about missions now.

ACKNOWLEDGMENTS

First of all, we want to thank Sojourn Church Midtown, for whom we originally wrote this book as fellow missions pastors. Thank you for shaping our understanding of the gospel, God's mission to the world, and the beauty of the historical church calendar. Thank you also for enabling us to make this accessible to more believers and churches around the world.

This project would not have been possible without the diligent work of the publishing team at the Upstream Collective: Larry McCrary, who heartily gave the green light; David McWhite, who edited richly and rapidly; Hayley Moss, who made it beautiful on short notice; and Jamie Chaplin and Jodie Sigrest, who pulled all the pieces together.

Bradley: I also want to recognize the blessing of my Antioch family and my Bell family—with all that we've got going on—giving me moments here and there to dream and to write with Nathan. Speaking of Nathan, he and I have done many crazy things together. Now we can add to the list that we co-authored a book. And maybe also that we coined the phrase "Lent and Missions." My friend, this has reminded me just how much we make a great team.

Nathan: Thanks to my wife, Sarah, who has journeyed with me through the seasons of personal suffering that have given meaning to the weightiness of Ash Wednesday and the glory of Easter Sunday. You are a gift to me, our children, and to our church. Thank you for your constant love, listening ear, and co-laboring in ministry.

ABOUT THE AUTHORS

Bradley Bell is the executive director of Upstream Equipping & Books. He has over twenty years of experience as a missionary, missions pastor, lead pastor, and missiologist. He is also the author of multiple Upstream books, including *The Sending Church Defined*. Bradley writes for numerous publications, which are compiled at brokenmissiology.org. He is married to Katie, and they have four daughters, all named after missionaries: Elisabeth, Charlotte, Anneliese, and Madeleine. They live in Louisville, Kentucky.

Nathan Sloan (*DMiss*, Southern Baptist Thelogical Seminary) is the executive director of Upstream Sending, a missions-sending organization focused on empowering the local church to send well. Nathan is also a pastor at Sojourn Church Midtown in Louisville, Kentucky, and is the author of *You Are Sent: Finding Your Place in God's Global Mission* and *Multisite Missions Leadership*. Nathan is married to Sarah, and they have two wonderful children, Asia and Jeremy.

OTHER BOOKS FROM UPSTREAM

Tradecraft: For the Church On Mission

Larry McCrary, Caleb Crider, Rodney Calfee, and Wade Stephens

The Western church world is abuzz with talk of being missional. Church leaders, conference speakers, and authors are weighing the merits of the attractional church movement of the past few decades, and where they find it lacking, prescribing changes in the way we need to approach our cultures with the Gospel. There has been a consensus shift among many churches, networks, and denominations to become more focused on mission. The result is a renewed interest in reaching the lost in our cities and around the world. The church, in many places in the Western world, is in fact returning to a biblical missional focus. Yet there is something still to be addressed in the process: the how. For centuries, God has called missionaries to cross cultures with the Gospel, and along the way, they have developed the necessary skill sets for a cultural translation of the good news. These skills need to be shared with the rest of the church in order to help them as well be effective missionaries. Tradecraft for the Church on Mission does exactly that. This book, in essence, pulls back the curtain on tools once accessible only to full-time Christian workers moving overseas, and offers them to anyone anywhere who desires to live missionally.

The Sending Church Defined
Bradley Bell

Purpose-driven church. Simple church. Organic church. Missional church. Deep church. Radical church. Transformational church. Total church. Sticky church. Tribal church. Mission-shaped church. Center church. Vertical church. Everyday church. Deliberate church. Gospel-centered church. Do we really need one more _____ church? "Yes!" say the collective of churches who consider themselves part of a growing movement called "sending church." It has proven itself as a term that is here to stay, but the meaning of it has been sadly mistaken. Many churches who call themselves sending churches are actually far from it. Some who are familiar with the term consider it just another missional trend. Others, upon first encounter think it speaks only to missiology. Sending church desperately needs clarity. That's precisely what this book is for.

It began with a gathering of sending churches who sought to answer the question, "What is a sending church?" They came up with a lengthy definition, and we then took almost a year to flesh out that definition one word at a time according to Scripture and scholarship. The goal was not just clarity, but to send a timely word to churches about reclaiming their birthright as the leaders in the Great Commission. After all, "A Sending church is a local community of Christ-followers who have made a covenant together to be prayerful, deliberate, and proactive in developing, commissioning, and sending their own members both locally and globally, often in partnership with other churches or agencies, and continuing to encourage, support, and advocate for them while making disciples cross-culturally and upon their return."

First 30 Daze: Practical Encouragement for Living Abroad Intentionally

Larry and Susan McCrary

Being a part of a non-profit sector allows us to live in and travel to many cities in the United States, as well as in Europe. As followers of Jesus, wherever we live or travel, our goal is to live out our faith in a different culture. It does not matter if you are a full-time vocational Christian worker, an international company employee, a student studying abroad, or a person who simply wants to live and work in another country — the first 30 days matter! The sooner you can get out the door, learn the culture, meet people, build relationships, and discover what God has in store for you, the sooner you will feel at home and love your new environment. Thirty topics and Scripture verses are introduced, as well as practical ways to apply what you've learned each day through a simple but fun application assignment. You may want to use the book as an individual devotional, with your family, or with a group. Regardless, it is short and practical so that you have plenty of time to get out and enjoy your new home.

Listen: How to Make the Most of Your Short-Term Mission Trip

Holding the Rope: How the Local Church Can Care for Its Sent Ones

The Market Space: Essential Relationships Between the Sending Church, Marketplace Worker, and Missionary Team

Receiving Sent Ones During Reentry: The Challenges of Returning "Home" and How Churches Can Help

Multisite Missions Leadership: The Challenges and Opportunities of Leading Missions at a Multisite Church

The Missionary Mama's Survival Guide: Compassionate Help for the Mothers of Cross-Cultural Workers

Order in bulk and get bulk pricing at: theupstreamcollective.org/books

For more resources, training, and consulting to empower local churches on mission, visit theupstreamcollective.org

Made in the USA
Monee, IL
01 February 2024